The Ultimate Guide to Orlando North Real Estate

Sara Hayes

Copyright © 2018 Sara Hayes

All rights reserved.

ISBN-13: 978-1984316066
ISBN-10: 1984316060

DEDICATION

Every client I have worked with has helped me to gain market knowledge and learn the tips and techniques to successfully sell homes.
I dedicate this book to you.

CONTENTS

	Forward	i
1	What is Orlando North?	3
2	Communities in Orlando North	7
3	House Hunting in Orlando North	15
4	Listing and Selling	21
5	Investment Properties	37
6	Calling Orlando North Home	41

FORWARD

Discover the hidden gem of Orlando North, a less touristy area of Central Florida with an abundance of natural beauty and recreational opportunities. Whether cycling, canoeing, golfing, or boating, this area offers it all. Home ownership in Orlando North is a wise investment, as the area continues to increase in popularity. Take a tour through the major cities within Orlando North, and then make note of the buying and selling tips specific to this region.

CHAPTER 1
WHAT IS ORLANDO NORTH?

Orlando North is located in Seminole County Florida. In 2015, county commissioners and tourism officials began to refer to the area north of downtown Orlando and Orange county as Orlando North Seminole County.

When living in Orlando North, residents enjoy a relaxing, natural setting that's just minutes from Orlando's top attractions. Miles of scenic rivers and acres of beautiful parks offer some of Florida's best natural attractions.

Residents and visitors frequent the Altamonte Mall for nearly 200 specialty shops, department stores and restaurants. Another must-see is Crane's Roost Park, where one can enjoy outdoor concerts, art shows and festivals. Or explore extensive nature trails at Lake Lotus Nature Park, which also has a fishing pier.

History buffs will love a tour of Longwood's charming Historical District, which offers 37 fascinating historical structures, including the Bradlee-McIntyre home. Discover natural wonders in over 1,500 acres of wilderness at Spring Hammock Preserve, and explore the waterways at Wekiva Island.

Frequent festivals and recreational opportunities occur in Oviedo throughout the year. A Great Day in the Country is a craft fair in November; Taste of Oviedo, highlighting the best of Oviedo occurs in the Spring; the farmers market is held on the first Saturday every month; and a fireworks show lights up the night on the 4th of July.

Lake Mary boasts one of Florida's best golf courses at the Timacuan Golf and Country Club, as well as the golf and tennis clubs at Heathrow. Enjoy miles of pristine nature and wildlife trails along the Cross Seminole Trail and the Florida National Scenic Trail. Lake Mary offers some of the most scenic areas of Orlando North.

Sanford is a gem of a city nestled along the St. John's River. The home of the Orlando Sanford International Airport and Amtrak Auto Train make Sanford a traveler's dream. In its Historic Downtown get a glimpse of late 1800s architecture, while enjoying shopping, dining and attractions.

Lake Monroe/St. John's River

CHAPTER 2
COMMUNITIES IN ORLANDO NORTH

ALTAMONTE SPRINGS

Retail options are plentiful in Altamonte Springs. Crane's Roost Park, Crane's Roost Lake, and the general area on State Road 436 east of Interstate 4 is known as the central area of the city. This is the area that borders Interstate 4, which is the main interstate highway for Central Florida connecting Daytona Beach, Orlando, and Tampa. An outdoor town center, called Uptown Altamonte, marks the central business district of the city. The lake is encircled by a one mile continuous walkway with covered seating areas and benches. The 45-acre park includes a European-style plaza, cobblestone pathways, themed lighting fixtures and a choreographed fountain show.

This city center incorporates large-scale apartment buildings and high rise condominiums. The development also includes mixed-use shops and retailers, while the park area has a square for weddings, festivals, and city holidays. The spot has become popular with Altamonte Springs residents, and attracts visitors from nearby Longwood, Casselberry, and Maitland.

During recent years, Altamonte Springs has been a host city to several local special events in the Orlando area, including Red, Hot, & Boom, a major annual fireworks festival that takes place every July 3rd in celebration of Independence Day. The Red, Hot, & Boom event draws over 100,000 local residents and visitors annually from the entire Central Florida area, which includes appearances and musical performances by nationally and internationally known entertainers, and is Central Florida's largest Independence Day Celebration.

Uptown Altamonte / Crane's Roost Park

LONGWOOD

Longwood is a city full of historic sites and quaint shopping areas. Longwood's Historic District encompasses roughly 190 acres and is located near the intersection of State Road 434 and County Road 427. It became part of the National Register of Historic Places in October 1990.

The Brandlee-McIntyre House is a Victorian cottage style house. On March 28, 1991, the house was added to the U.S. National Registrar of Historic Places. The Bradlee-McIntyre House was built in 1885 for noted Boston architect Nathanial Jeremiah Bradlee and family. It is the only surviving "cottage" in Orange and Seminole counties, a Queen Anne style three-story, 13 room winter vacation house featuring an octagonal tower and "ginger-bread" trim typical of homes from the Victorian Period.

Historic Longwood

OVIEDO

Oviedo is a city to the northeast of downtown Orlando. Originally pronounced O-vee-a-dough, the city has an informal sister city relationship established with Oviedo, Spain. Residential communities including single family homes, townhouses, and apartments are being developed. In addition, Oviedo is expanding its downtown area on approximately 50 acres.

Oviedo is also within close proximity to the University of Central Florida. Professors and university staff enjoy a short drive to campus, and students have apartment options for off campus living. Religious, civic, and social groups round out the city and fosters a hometown atmosphere.

Oviedo City Limits

LAKE MARY

Lake Mary has never lost its focus of promoting a sense of community where people can live, work and play in a safe and friendly environment...that's part of the reason Lake Mary is still one of the fastest growing areas in Central Florida. Just off Interstate 4, the city continues to be a choice location for high tech businesses, many of which spend considerable time and money searching for the right place. Among other things Lake Mary is known for its well planned residential communities, excellent schools, prominent businesses.

A wide variety of housing choices are available in and around Lake Mary. Young professionals will find an array of affordable apartments, luxury condos and rental properties. Growing families will find the quiet community neighborhoods a safe and inviting place to call home. For those looking towards retirement there are upscale golf course communities and active retirement communities all within a few minutes of I-4.

In 2018, a new development called Griffin Farms Town Center opens near downtown Lake Mary and offers high density residential mixed with grocery, retail and dining. The new area is known as "Mid-town" Lake Mary and is replacing a decades old Griffin cattle ranch.

Downtown Lake Mary

SANFORD

Known as the "Historic Waterfront Gateway City," Sanford sits on the southern shore of Lake Monroe at the head of navigation on the St. Johns River. Sanford is home to the Seminole State College of Florida and the Central Florida Zoo. Its downtown attracts tourists with shops, restaurants, a marina, and a lakefront walking trail. The Orlando Sanford International Airport functions as the secondary commercial airport for international and domestic carriers in the Orlando metro area.

An unincorporated area west of I-4 shares the Sanford post office and mailing address. Some refer to the area as Lake Forest, although it is not designated as such by the Census Bureau or any municipality authorities. The trailhead of the Seminole Wekiva Trail is located in this unincorporated area. The trail is 14 miles long and stretches from Sanford to Altamonte Springs.

Seminole Wekiva Trail

CHAPTER 3
HOUSE HUNTING IN ORLANDO NORTH

Orlando North is a wonderland of housing opportunities. Community features often include guarded gates, large resort-style pools, workout facilities, recreational areas, tennis courts and golf courses. Once a buyer is ready to start the house hunting process, a few recommendations should be noted.

FINANCES

Home ownership has been viewed as the cornerstone of financial stability. The home provides both physical shelter, fosters friendships and community ties for a lifetime, and also appreciates in value over time. Taxes benefits are available to homeowners paying mortgage interest. Home owners enjoy the freedom of decorating, remodeling, and other renovation projects often prohibited to renters.

Buying is not for everyone, and several factors should be considered. Given the buyer's particular circumstance, length of time in home should be estimated. Three to five years? Ten? Longer? If the answer is three years or more, then buying real estate is a smart move. Paying rent year after year is only making the landlord wealthy for the long term.

What does the buyer's financial picture look like? Are there enough funds saved for a significant down payment? Ideally, a buyer should have 20% saved for a down payment, however, other options do exist. In addition to the down payment, closing costs from the lender and title fees will also come into play. Both the lender and title company can give the buyer estimates up front when a property is pursued.

Income, debt, assets and job verification will be calculated to approve the buyer for a home mortgage. The interest rate and other terms will be disclosed to the buyer, including a realistic price range.

SETTING CRITERIA

Once the lender has provided a budget for the purchase price, the house criteria can be set and the search can begin. What is the property type - condo, townhouse, or single family home? Zero lot line, 1 acre, or more? Number of bedrooms, bathrooms, and garage spaces? Age of home, deed restrictions, HOA requirements?

SEARCH

Buyers can use numerous methods to house hunt. Public websites such as Zillow, Trulia, and Realtor.com allow buyers to anonymously browse homes for sale. Websites pull information from various sources, and may not be the most reliable source of information due to delays in the information feed.

Private searches can be established through Realtors and the local multiple list system (MLS). MLS provides accurate information updated by the minute. Buyers receive automatic notifications of new listings, price adjustments, and status changes.

VIEWING HOMES

Once a buyer has a reasonable list of homes to view, the preview showings can be scheduled. The goal of the preview is to get a quick view of a series of homes, eliminate those with "deal breaker" issues, and identify homes which meet most of the criteria.

ANALYZING COMPARABLES

With a home or homes identified as a match to the buyer, recent sales in the neighborhood should be analyzed. House sale histories can be found on the county website, or through the MLS system. The more recent the sale and the closer the proximity to the subject property the better. The homes are better comparisons if they have similar features, age, and number of bedrooms and bathrooms. A rule of thumb in comparing homes is the price per square foot, although many other factors should be considered when determining a home's value. Homes that were sold short or foreclosed on will have a lower price per square foot. Homes with extensive updates will have a higher price per square foot.

MAKING AN OFFER

A standard sale contract can be used to submit an offer based on price, down payment, contingencies, loan terms, and escrow period. Once presented, the sellers can accept, reject, or return a counter offer. This process can take a few hours, or a few days. Parties may not come to an agreement, and then try again at a later date. As long as both parties agree to the terms, almost anything can be negotiated in a contract.

ESCROW PERIOD

The time period from accepted contract to the day of closing is called the escrow period. Within the first few days of the escrow period, the buyer's earnest money is deposited at the title company and held until close. The earnest money will then be applied as a credit on the buyer's closing statement.

Title insurance provides the buyer with assurance that the house has a clear title, no liens or encumbrances that could jeopardize their claim to the property. The lender is also interested in the property having clear title. In the circumstance of foreclosure, the bank will have the first claim to the property. The title company will also manage title-related documents, notarized signatures, and any liens on the property. The transfer of ownership is recorded in county records. Once the information is made public, it can be viewed by anyone with a need to know about the transaction and new owner information.

OCCUPANCY

Once funds have transferred to the seller, the buyer obtains the keys and possession of the property. The buyer can immediately occupy the home, or take some time to remodel, repaint, or decorate.

CHAPTER 4
LISTING AND SELLING

PREPARING HOME FOR SHOWINGS

Selling a home is a business transaction. It is a professional interaction between a buyer and a seller. The probability of success of this interaction is affected greatly by the first impression. A clean and organized home is a must. The goal of the preparation is to get it sold faster and for a higher price than simply putting it on the market as is. Try to overcome buyers' objections before they have even entered the home. Depending on the amount of work needed, it may take a week or two to prepare the home for sale.

Small repairs and carpet cleaning/replacement should occur prior to listing. A to-do list and a carpet allowance is a less favorable first impression. Clean floors are especially important in a vacant home.

Cleaning and staging a home like a model is the key to a successful home sale. Major home builders across the nation have spent hundreds of thousands of dollars researching how to market a home. They know how to grab a buyer's attention and create a lasting impression on them. Model homes are clean, depersonalized, and odor free.

Décor and staging – Dora Lisa Ferretti

Haven't been to a model home recently? Take an hour to go by a new community with a model home and observe why they are so successful at selling dozens of houses within a year. Not your style? Doesn't feel lived in? There is a difference between living in a home and selling a home. Increase the lived-in look with fresh flowers on a table, fresh fruit in the kitchen, and several lamps to soften the light in each room. Even a small room can be made to look larger with the correct furnishings, wall color, and lighting.

If a home has foul odors, the buyers will always remember the home that way – "the curry condo," "cat poop house," "the ashtray." This includes pet odors, this morning's bacon, and last weekend's beach towel. Lingering cigarette smoke odor may need to be professionally treated.

Decluttering the home will also help to market it. Renting a storage unit for a few months will allow buyers to see more of the closets, cabinets, and rooms during their showing.

Closets, especially in the master bedroom, have become increasingly important to buyers. Setting the closet up like a boutique is ideal. Clothes on hangers should be spaced apart and hang freely. Remove most items from the floor to make the closet appear larger. Don't kid yourself with closed doors. Buyers will open doors, drawers, cabinets, refrigerators, ovens and dishwashers.

PRICING HOME FOR SALE

A home's listing price can make or break the sale. Therefore, research should include many factors. Past sales for the neighborhood, or "comps" is the starting point for the pricing strategy. It is rare to find an identical match, but many communities share floorplans and can be compared. Do not confuse active listings with past sales. Active listings do not determine the value of other homes. Active listings are simply the competition. They are also indicators of what *isn't* selling.

Sellers should avoid overpricing the home because selling is not a priority. An overpriced listing typically sits on the market for months. Showings often begin the day the house is listed, resulting in dozens of potential buyers coming through for showings. A better strategy would be to wait until the time is right and price the home close to market value.

Leave some room for negotiation, but not too much. The list price should give both the buyer and seller room to maneuver. The price should feel like a win-win for all parties.

First impressions are everything when selling a home. The first two weeks on the market are the most crucial to success. During these initial days the home is exposed to all active buyers. If the price is perceived as too high, this initial audience will be lost and the listing becomes stale.

NEGOTIATING AN OFFER

When the house is priced at its sweet spot, an offer will soon occur. The buyer should expect the seller to counter offer. The first offer may be low, and it is important for the seller to not take the offer personally. The initial offer gets the ball in play and a successful series of counter offers will result in an accepted sales contract.

At times, an offer is so low and poorly considered that it should not be given a response. However, most of the time it is best to respond to offers. By refusing to counter the seller is adding a little slap to the buyer's ego. The buyer may not submit another offer, and the buyer's maximum price will never be known. A low offer may occur for several reasons. The buyer may be unfamiliar with the market and local culture, and may believe greater price reductions are commonplace. It may be in the buyer's background or culture to negotiate aggressively.

Nothing is more destructive to the negotiation process than the adversarial style. Professional negotiators try to preserve the relationship between the parties. The goal is not to reach an impasse in which neither the seller's nor buyer's needs are met. Sometimes buyers include a note with their offer explaining why the house is not worth what they are asking, pointing out deficiencies, etc. No one can read a note criticizing their house without a defensive reaction.

In the same vein, the seller's attitude toward the buyer can be effective in solidifying their interest in the home. The negotiation process usually begins with some degree of distrust between buyer and seller. The goal is to move in the direction of trust as quickly as possible.

Sometimes there is no choice but to work with an adversarial buyer. Their strategy includes: emotional statements, snide remarks, defensive arguments, threats to terminate, ego involvement, and stated positioning. Creative solutions are not likely to be found in this environment.

Working with a combative style buyer requires the seller to control his/her own emotions. An angry or defensive response will escalate the negotiation into a no-win battle. Arguing certain points strengthens each side's opinion and takes the negotiation process off course. All offers should be in writing. The counter offer should be as attractive as possible. Allow for some "wins," such as closing date, or seller paid closing costs. At the end of the day, the buyer is a qualified individual who may be able satisfy the seller's goals.

INSPECTION

Within the first 10 – 15 days of the accepted contract, the buyer will order a full building inspection. An inspector examines the house thoroughly for non-functioning systems, damages, and repairs that may be needed. The detailed report forms the basis for continuing with the purchase, renegotiating the sale price, allowing the seller to make repairs, or for pulling out of the sale. A home inspection is recommended on purchases of new construction as well as re-sales and is a critical component of an escrow timeline.

A home inspector climbs onto the roof, pokes at the foundation, and crawls into attic space looking for water condensation or penetration. On homes in hurricane zones, roof trusses will be examined to be sure they're connected to the frame as per code. Walls are examined for leakage or mold. Floor cracks are noted, as is separation from the baseboards. The ceilings, especially around electrical fixtures, must be clear of any signs of water leakage.

Close inspection of the exterior may reveal where additional caulking is needed to prevent water seepage. Broken seals on glass, deteriorating tread steps, decking and settlement cracks are a few of the items that require professional repair. Even the garage door is tested whether it's electronic or manual.

The roof is examined closely for loose shingles or tiles, and the flashing is tested for tightness. Tree limbs touching the house provide a passageway for rodents and also can threaten the house during violent storms. Gutter debris is noted, and all drains are tested for a tight connection to the house. Skylights and chimneys also are examined for proper sealants.

All piping is tested, including drains, vents and waste systems. Water ingress and egress is examined, as are the interior fuel and water distributors and the sump pump, if present. All drains are examined for signs of leakage, mineral deposits and the fitting of proper filtering apparatus. Inspectors may test the water for bacteria.

All the electrical components are examined to ensure they fit and are operating safely. Conductors, grounding equipment and distribution panels are tested for efficient operation. The location of smoke and carbon monoxide detectors also is noted in the inspection report.

The entire heating and air conditioning system is tested to verify it's in working condition, and the appropriate filters are examined for accumulation. Supply pipes are examined for corrosion. Chimneys must be clear of bird nests, and the chimney frame, whether it's brick or made of other components, is to be sound.

Attic crawl space insulation and vapor retarders are noted on the inspection report. All venting fans that aren't working also are included. Under-floor insulation, if accessible through the basement, also is examined for deterioration.

Doors, floors, stairways, counters, cabinetry, and the number of windows are all cited on the inspection report along with notes on any items that don't function as they should. This also includes testing of all interior appliances that are built-in or included in the purchase contract.

APPRAISAL

A real estate appraisal is an opinion of value,

provided by a professional with certain prerequisite training and experience and licensed by the state in which he or she operates in. This opinion is based on an investigation of the subject property, the neighborhood, as well as market conditions and appropriate comparable sales. The analysis of the foregoing data is then condensed and reconciled into that opinion of value.

There are two primary appraisal methods for residential property, the sales comparison approach and the cost approach. In the sales comparison approach, the appraiser compares the property with three or four similar homes that have sold in the area, often called comparables, or comps. The analysis considers specific components, such as lot size, square footage of finished and unfinished space, style and age of house, as well as other features such as garages and fireplaces.

The cost approach is used more for new property and is based on reproduction costs. The appraiser estimates the cost to replace the structure on the property if it were destroyed. The appraiser then looks at land value and depreciation to determine the property's worth.

The appraiser gathers information for the appraisal report from a number of sources, but the process often begins with a physical inspection of the property inside and out. Additionally, the appraiser may look at county courthouse records and recent reports from the local real estate MLS.

The appraisal report generally includes:

- an explanation of how the appraiser determined the value of the property

- the size and condition of the house and other permanent fixtures, along with a description of any improvements that have been made and the materials used

- statements regarding serious structural problems, such as wet basements and cracked foundations

- notes about the surrounding area, such as new or established development, rural acreage, and so on

- an evaluation of recent market trends of the area that may affect the value

- a comparative market analysis that supports the appraisal

- maps, photographs and sketches

A common misunderstanding is that the appraisal amount is only for the house itself. In fact, the figure appraises the total value of the home and any other permanent structures, along with the land that the house is built on. This appraisal figure also determines the loan amount the buyer can obtain to buy the property.

In some cases the appraisal comes in lower than the contract price. How can buyers and sellers can recover from a low appraisal?

First, take a look at what may have caused the low appraisal. It might be due to factors that the homeowner could correct, such as repairs or maintenance. If that's the case, the appraiser may be willing to take a second look and adjust the appraisal accordingly.

Ordering a second appraisal is always an option. This may be a good idea if the first appraiser is inexperienced or unfamiliar with the area where the property is located. It's possible that a second appraisal will uncover mistakes the first appraiser made.

From the lender's standpoint, however, the mortgage transaction is at a standstill until something else happens. Perhaps the seller will lower the asking price, or the homebuyer may be willing to increase their cash down payment. It's possible that both buyer and seller can negotiate compromises that will satisfy the lender.

If, however, negotiations fall through and the appraisal is still too far below what the bank is willing to finance, then there's no choice but to cancel the transaction. An appraisal contingency is a standard item on Florida real estate purchase contracts, and allows for the contract to be cancelled at this point. Earnest money is to be returned to the buyer and the seller is released from the contract and can relist.

A home appraisal is more than just another cost added to the buyer's bottom line. It's a protection for everyone involved in the home-buying process.

CHAPTER 5
INVESTMENT PROPERTIES

Investment properties are prevalent in Florida, and specifically in Orlando North. Whether purchased as a rental or as a quick flip, a house or condo can be a wise investment, as long as it is done pragmatically and with caution. Unlike buying a home to live in, investment property purchases should be void of emotion.

In general, the best investment property for beginners is a residential, single-family home, a townhouse or condo. Townhouses and condos are low maintenance because the community association will cover many of the external repairs, leaving the investor to only deal with interior repairs. Single-family homes tend to attract longer-term renters in the form of families and couples.

Renters in the Sunshine State are willing to pay a higher price to have a place to call home in Florida. Therefore, investors purchasing rental properties quickly find out that the constant inflow of cash can come from vacationing families, retirees, and college students. The variety in the local population, warm weather and above average monthly rent contribute to the investor's cash return. The average rental home stays on the market for less than one month.

Never dreamed of being a landlord? This isn't the only way to collect passive income through real estate investment. A management team can be hired to handle the direct dealings with tenants. This allows investors to still benefit from this secondary source of income without it becoming a time consuming activity.

Looking to flip? Cosmetically challenged houses that can be beautified and sold without a huge investment of time, effort, or repair and renovation costs are found in abundance in Orlando North. When purchasing a quick flip opportunity, the goal is to make the property impeccably clean and well-maintained, something all home buyers want.

A home with old carpet and paisley wallpaper may be easy, and cheap, to update. Other home repairs to tackle might include replacing old kitchen linoleum, and replacing hollow doors with six-panel doors throughout the home. A house that has water damage, mold, needs a roof replacement, or needs rewiring, requires some serious time and cash to update and sell.

A written budget is required to identify what improvements can be included in the project. Certain home improvements will increase the selling price of the house more than others. The kitchen is the most important room in the house. Most experts recommend focusing on kitchen remodeling, and then look into bathroom redesign. Analyze the cost to renovate the kitchen in order to make it appealing for future buyers.

Ensure the price of the home is *below* its value in the local market. The instant equity will give the project an up-front financial boost, while helping to offset the closing costs of the real estate transaction. Investors are advised to buy the worst house in a great neighborhood, versus the best house in a lousy neighborhood.

Ultimately, the real estate investment may involve both renting and flipping. If possible, it would be best to purchase a home, do the necessary repairs and then expect to hold on to it for six to twelve months. During this period of time the house can be rented out in order to keep an income coming in from the investment. Time is usually of the essence, and the investment should continue to increase in value. Each investment project may have different opportunities and outcomes.

CHAPTER 6

CALLING ORLANDO NORTH HOME

Rivers, wilderness areas, orange groves and sandy beaches are all within an hour drive of Orlando North. Kayak, hike, skydive and swim all year round. Moss-covered oaks and sabal palms define the landscape as deer bears, peacocks, cranes, and flocks of exotic birds abound.

Of course, the amusement parks and cruise ports are also nearby. A 15 minute drive to Disney, or an hour drive to Port Canaveral makes enjoying a day at Disney or a Caribbean cruise much more affordable. Kennedy Space Center is another close attraction with educational day tours and frequent rocket launches.

Kennedy Space Center

How about the weather? One of the area's biggest draws is the year-round sunny, mild weather. In keeping with the "Sunshine State", Orlando North maintains a comfortable average annual temperature of 72 degrees and a mostly dry climate from October to May.

Whether relocating from elsewhere, looking for a second home, or already rooted in Orlando North, the real estate and community resources are plentiful.

Wekiva River

ABOUT THE AUTHOR

Sara Hayes prides herself on exceptional customer service. As an experienced Realtor, Sara shares her market and contract knowledge with her clients while allowing them to set the pace for the home search. Sara and her husband live in Sanford and she specializes in the Orlando North area. Her daughter is active in school and sports and Sara has many community connections. Sara also makes referrals nationwide to buyers and sellers who want to be connected with top producing agents in their particular city. Locally, Sara works with first time home buyers, empty-nesters, and anyone in between. When you are looking for a Realtor who will listen, advise, and guide rather than push, call Sara Hayes.

www.ingramcontent.com/pod-product-compliance
Lightning Source LLC
Chambersburg PA
CBHW040241220526
45473CB00001B/322